Thoughts of a Closet Freak
The Reflections of My Desires

Lisa Renee Hutchins

Copyright 2023 Lisa Renee Hutchins

ISBN: 978-1-959446-13-2

Author

Lisa Renee Hutchins

Cover Design by

SuburbanBuzz.com LLC

Interior Design by

Moyer Productions Co. LLC

Editing by

Helen Muriithi

Formatting by

Farhan Shahid and Lisa Hutchins

All rights reserved. No part of this book may be reproduced or transmitted in any form or by any means, electronic or mechanical, including photocopying or recording, or by any information storage or retrieval system, without written permission from the publisher.

Published by SuburbanBuzz.com LLC

Contents

Inspiration i
Dear Closet Freaks ii

Opening the Door

All She Knows 1
First Sight 3
Curiosity Consumes the Cat 5
Little Pictures Have Big Ears 6
The Box of Wonder 8
Unfamiliar Sensations 11
The Secret Touch 12
Hidden Addiction 14
Butterflies a Flutter 15
Prince in the Night 16
Loves Transes 19

Fantasy Land

Magical Moments 22
The Waiting Game 24
Boomerang 26
Passionate Raindrops 27

The Way 29
Do You? 32

Gifts of Seduction

Magnetic 34
Scents of Attraction 36
Contained 38
The Cookie Jar 40
No Turning Back 41
Sangria 44
Gummy Necklace 48
Seductive Feathers and a Blindfold 50
Intertwined 54
Assume the Position 56
Chocolate Painting Pleasure 58
Classy Cuffs 61
The Only Benefit 63
Together in the Warmth 64
Candle Wax of Love 67
Thirsty Thrill 71
Water Works 73
A Movie and Popcorn 75
In the Midst of You 76

Going Up...80

Behind the Satin Bow 85

A Night of Seduction 87

Lunchtime Sounds 93

Something New 95

Secrets from Within

Unexpected Interruption 98

Caught in the Middle..101

The Gaze from Within 102

A Man I Once Craved...104

Love's Shackled Prisoner 106

Shattered Glass..108

Trusting the One We Follow...110

Callus 112

Not Enough..113

The Silent Daily Reminders..114

The Wedge of Life 116

The Lonely World of Boundaries..120

One to Remember..121

Exhale 122

Lioness in the Shadows 124

Untouchable 128

Can't Wait..130

Unforgettable

Unexpected Connection 134

Undercover Love 136

The Touch 138

Reminiscing 139

Until Next Time 140

The Heart's Assumption 142

After Thoughts

Double Standard 144

Hard Lesson Learned 145

Forgiveness is Freedom 147

Be True 148

Sexual Soul Ties 150

The Morning Drive Home 152

Sex vs Love 154

Two Halves Don't Make a Whole 155

Single Satisfaction 156

Saving Yourself 157

The True Love of Another 158

About the Author

Thank You

Inspiration

My inspiration for this book is to share my inner thoughts on what it is like to discover, explore and enjoy sex, and intimacy as a woman.

We, as women, are not taught to share our needs, wants, and sexual desires. We are taught to keep quiet and follow someone's lead, which may not be the fit we need to be our true selves.

Love, intimacy, and sex all play different roles in our sexual journey. Our first exposure to this may be the feelings we get when we see people connecting on TV or when we like someone for the first time. From there, we start opening the doors to what the world has in store. We fantasize about what our first time will be like with the person we daydream about. We start experimenting to understand the feeling of intertwining and how to bring pleasure to one another.

Then, all of a sudden, we discover the gifts of seduction, how it creates the secrets we hide within, and teaches us to set boundaries for where our journey leads us.

Dear Closet Freaks

Hello, my closet freaks! We are professionals, possibly wearing suits in an office or running our own businesses from home, working by day, but by night we embark on a path to exploring the unknown.

Then, all of a sudden, we begin to discover the gifts of seduction, how it creates the secrets we keep, and teaches us that we all have limits.

Some of us feel alive and confident in our skin and are not afraid to act on our curiosity and desires. We feel the need to be fulfilled and cherished for our vulnerability to explore.

I hope you see yourself in this book and know that you are not the only women with a high sex drive who keeps it in the closet only for special people who can unlock the doors.

Opening the Door

Opening the Door

All She Knows

Every morning,

The little girl wakes up

To her mother's sweet voice and warm hugs

Showering her with love to start her day

She stumbles down the hallway

Still half asleep, rubbing her eyes

Her father walks around the corner

With his arms opened wide

She welcomes his embrace

As he smiles with laughter in his voice

He leans down to kiss her on the forehead

Reminding her that "Every day is a good day"

Thoughts of a Closet Freak

This affection is the love

She knows how to show and receive

Not knowing, that as she grows

Life has undiscovered doors of affection

Waiting for her to open

Opening the Door

First Sight

A little girl is woken from her sleep

By unfamiliar sounds

She slowly gets out of bed

Tip-toeing quietly to the living room

To see what her parents were watching

As she peaks around the corner

She sees two people on the screen

Naked and moving together

They were making strange noises

That were getting louder

She trips over a toy

As she sneaks to get a closer look

Thoughts of a Closet Freak

Her mother and father immediately turn around
With surprised looks on their faces
Her father pauses the show
While her mother rushes over, trying to block her view

She turns her daughter around
Walking her back to her room
Quickly changing the subject

She tucks her daughter back into bed
Kissing her good night

The little girl lies there wondering,
"What were they "doing"?"
"Why can't I see it?"
Igniting a forbidden curiosity to explore

Curiosity Consumes the Cat

In the beginning,

The innocence of a child's mind is pure

Not intrigued by intimacy

Until one day,

They see or hear the passion

Only adults get to see in the dark

The child begins to snoop around

Trying to find a glimpse of the secrets

Hidden behind closed doors

Thoughts of a Closet Freak

Little Pictures Have Big Ears

Her parents invite the family over for a BBQ
Cousins, aunties, uncles, and the grandparents
She knows this is the perfect time to eavesdrop

As all the uncles show up
They go outside, where her dad is cooking

She stands at the sliding glass door, listening
But right away, her uncles see her, calling her over
She smiles, giving them all hugs

She stands there, offering to help her dad
He kisses her on the head
Telling her to go into the house with her mom

Opening the Door

She goes to the kitchen to help her mother
All her aunties are in there laughing and carrying on

The aunties give her hugs and ask how she is doing
Then her mother tells her to go play with the kids
Because they are talking "grown folks' business"

As she walks down the hall
She wonders, "What is so secretive about "grown folk's business"

Thoughts of a Closet Freak

The Box of Wonder

She knew her brother had secrets

Always telling her to stay out of his room

Today, her parents were running late

And her brother just left for basketball practice

She has a small window of time to go through his stuff

So, she takes the chance

Carefully looking everywhere

Trying not to make a mess

Opening draws

Shuffling through the closet

And under the bed

Opening the Door

She could not find anything
Before leaving his room in disappointment
She checks under his bed one more time

This time she moves his blanket
There was a box labeled "Don't Open"

The adrenalin rushes through her body
Intriguing her curiosity to see what was inside
Quickly taking off the lid
Her eyes were stunned

The magazines were filled with beautiful, naked ladies
Posing with their bodies in unfamiliar positions

There were DVDs with naked men and women
Connecting in ways she never saw before

Thoughts of a Closet Freak

Her heart starts beating fast
The more she looks through the box

She lost track of time
All of a sudden, the garage door opens

She franticly put everything back in the box
Placing the blanket perfectly under his bed
Closing his door quietly
As she runs into her room

Unfamiliar Sensations

The images of sex

Brings tingling sensations

A warmth and wetness

Never felt before

A spark of curiosity

To see more

A hungry craving

To explore

The Secret Touch

In the dark

Her hand slides down

Over and around her breasts

Bushing across her nipples

Triggering a pleasurable sensation

Intrigued by the feeling

Her hand goes lower

Softly touching her kitty cat

With a curiosity to learn what's within

Feeling a comforting warmth trickling from her body

Opening the Door

Her fingers are gliding back up
Until she accidentally hits a spot at the top of her kitty
This feeling is intensely sensitive

The faster she moves up and down
The better it feels

She grabs the top of her blanket with her other hand
As she covers her mouth
Muffling the sounds of ecstasy

The feeling of release and relaxations overcomes her
With a craving to feel that explosive energy again

Hidden Addiction

The feelings of intimacy
Control her thoughts
Creating an intense anticipation
For the moment she will feel relief gain

Changing her sense of time
Increasing the desire
To make alone time a priority

Exploring herself
Enjoying secret moments of pleasure
Without getting caught

Butterflies a Flutter

On her way to history class
Her crush comes down the hallway
Laughing with his friends

His presence makes her body tingle
As the butterflies began fluttering in her stomach
She wonders, "Maybe today he will notice me"

The closer he gets
The more profound the fluttering becomes
She collects her nervousness, walking confidently towards him

Time suddenly stands still
As he glances her way, smiling
The butterflies began fluttering out of control
Bringing a beaming smile to her face

Thoughts of a Closet Freak

Prince in the Night

The pink satin gown was elegant
Flowing effortlessly as she walks in the door

Her brown hair was up, revealing her neckline
Accented with a dainty tiara
Sparkling as the diamonds reflect the light

Her white satin gloves and sleek high heels
Bring a touch of wonder to her presence

She stands on the side of the dance floor with her friends
Patiently waiting to see the man of the evening

The music brings her out of her shell
Filling the room with a welcoming energy

Opening the Door

As a slow song starts playing

The mood changes

She turns around to leave the dance floor

And there he is

Smiling with a twinkle in his eyes

He politely extends his hand

Inviting her to dance

She smiles in surprise, graciously accepting

As he holds her close

The smell of his cologne draws her into his chest

The comfort of his conversation intrigues her interest

As they gaze into each other's eyes

Gliding as one across the dance floor

Thoughts of a Closet Freak

The song comes to an end
But the dance with her prince
Seemed like an eternity

Loves Transes

As she watches the sunset from her bedroom
window She catches herself daydreaming
Reminiscing about her prince in the night

The twinkle in his eyes
His smile that melted her heart
The happiness knowing that he chose her

The joy of being in his arms
Moving as one to the music
Smelling the cologne on his chest
As she embraced his warm body

A passionate feeling overcomes her body
With a smile she cannot erase
Spinning around blissfully with her eyes closed

Thoughts of a Closet Freak

She opens her eyes

Coming back to reality

With the glow of the sunset brings a warmth to her heart

In hopes that they will be together once again

Fantasy Land

Thoughts of a Closet Freak

Magical Moments

Nestled in bed

Under a warm down blanket

With red LED lights aglow

She replays their first kiss

Over and over again

The soothing beat of the song

Gliding them together in perfect harmony

The magic she felt in his presence

As he took the lead

Dancing his way into her heart

Fantasy Island

The smell of his cologne

That remains on her dress

Causing her attraction to grow stronger

The comfort she felt

Embraced in his arms

Never wanting it to end

The closeness pulling her in

As he kissed her good-bye

Making time stand still

A magical moment

That will never get old

Replaying forever

Thoughts of a Closet Freak

The Waiting Game

When will he be mine?

Today, as the morning sun rises,

Tomorrow, as the afternoon winds blow,

Or never, as the night grows colder with emptiness.

What will he do?

Be a ghost in the night,

Stay around for a moment,

Or be a rock of stability.

What will he whisper?

Broken promises,

Honorable truths,

Or comforting reassurance.

Fantasy Island

How do I know if his love is real?

Through his actions,

The expressions of unconditional love,

Or his willingness to grow as one.

Thoughts of a Closet Freak

Boomerang

Parting ways

Makes the heart grow founder

Building stronger feelings

Connecting two lovers

Counting down the days

Until life

Bring them back together

Once again

Passionate Raindrops

The rain slowly trickles down our faces
As we kiss each other in the moonlight

Your arms delicately embrace me
As we try to say goodbye

Then you unexpectedly pick me up
I held on in surprise

But it intrigued a part of me
I don't often share

When we got to my car
Your body confidently presses against mine

Thoughts of a Closet Freak

The rain starts coming down faster
Intensifying our feelings

Your hand firmly massages my back
As I hold you close

You gently bite my neck
Sparking my desire to return the favor

We both fill with undeniable passion
Knowing that was not our intent

We finally part ways, but both wanting more

As I drove home
The smell of your cologne was intertwined with my sweater
Bringing a smile to my face
Making me yearn for your touch once more

The Way

The way you look at me makes my body melt

As I yearn for your touch

My mind fantasizes

About what I want to do to you

I gently touch your hands

Pulling you close

I kiss your soft lips

Caressing your smooth back

I softly take off your shirt

While I kiss your muscular chest

Thoughts of a Closet Freak

Your heart begins to race

As you moan for more

You are mesmerized by my touch

As I caress your body

Removing your jeans

The sensation intensifies

As I slowly climb on top

Penetrating you slowly

I massage my chest

Staring into your eyes

The temperature rises as we reach ecstasy

Fantasy Island

I blink

Look away

And reality appears

But my fantasy

Still remains

Do You?

Do you think about me?

Do you miss my smile?

Do you miss our laughter?

Do you think about the times we shared?

Do you yearn to hear my voice?

Do you count the days till we touch?

Do you have plans for our future?

Do you want a family?

Do you want to grow old with me?

Gifts of Seduction

Thoughts of a Closet Freak

Magnetic

A man walks into the room with a sleek, smooth confidence
Dressed in a sexy black suit
Smiling with a contagious energy

Standing with a purpose
Suddenly and unexpectedly
He spots the woman of his dreams

She is beautiful, confident, and full of joy
The glow from her aura steals his heart

Slightly intimidated by her presence
He waits patiently for an opportunity

When their eyes meet

The attraction is instant

As he smoothly approaches her

Their laughter is undeniable

Their conversation is natural

Their connection is magnetic

Igniting an unbreakable destiny

She is going to be his forever

Scents of Attraction

When he opens the door
Subtle vanilla candles secretly float through the air
Bring a sense of comfort and safety

When he softly kisses her
A soothing cologne sent catches her attention
Sparking a fire inside

A fresh bouquet of red roses
Sitting in the center of the table
Brings a twinkle to her eyes

As they sit at the table set for two

A sizzling steak and potato entree awaits

Igniting her taste buds

He invites her to pray with him

Building a tiny fire

That is starting to burn in their hearts

Intertwining their minds

As love fills the air

Contained

The butterflies of passion are growing inside

Making my heart flutter

In anticipation of seeing him again

To feel this feeling

I have never felt

I start losing myself in his presence

In his arms

When his lips touch mine

My body starts getting wet in places

Only I explore

When he gets close, I hesitate

Keeping myself guarded

Trying to contain my desires

Waiting for the day

When I am ready to set my butterflies free

Thoughts of a Closet Freak

The Cookie Jar

The cookies in the jar are forbidden

Only to be eaten

At a certain time and place

There is a limit

To who gets a cookie

And who does not

Sometimes curiosity about the taste

Overtakes one's judgment

Or proves the strength of one's willpower

The cookie jar is waiting

What will you do?

No Turning Back

The first taste of the cookie
Is a savory experience

Quickly, you look around from left to right
Making sure no one is in sight

With a slight tremble of excitement
You open the jar

Anticipating what type of cookies await
Reaching in swiftly to grab one

Pulling out a cookie
Holding it in amazement
While you quietly close the lid

Thoughts of a Closet Freak

Sitting down in front of the counter

Holding the cookie in your sweaty hands

Looking at the round shape

Slightly squeezing it to test the softness

No longer resisting the urge

Closing your eyes

You take a huge bite

Crumbs fall onto your pants

While the warm chocolate

Sticks to the corners of your mouth

Stroking your taste buds with an ecstasy

You never endured before

Craving the next bit, and the next

Until… It's all gone

Filling you with a desire for more

Anticipating the next time

You sneak into the cookie jar again

Sangria

Our Sangrias swirl with fruit and ice
As we casually sip our drinks
Laughing endlessly

The happiness in my glass
Slowly trickles down my throat
Filling my stomach with trust and compassion

The ice cubes began to melt
The more glasses we share
The warmer your innocent touch became
Never hinting more than a soothing connection

Our evening was coming to an end
As I get ready to leave
You softly grab my hand
Guiding me into your arms

Gently kissing
We slowly caress each other
As we move toward the couch

You sit down
Guiding me towards you
I gently straddle you
Holding you close
Massaging your smooth shoulders

You stare into my eyes
Connecting with my soul
The gentle observation of our bodies
Feels genuine and true

Thoughts of a Closet Freak

As you sit back to watch me
You capture my feelings

Your right hand slowly moves up my chest
Lightly grabbing my neck

I caress your hand, and lean back
Your left hand rotates my hips
Pressing your body between my legs

You ignite my need for your affection
Your patient touch opens my heart

The intensity between us is undeniable
As we reluctantly untangle

The sensation of our skin irresistibly reconnects

Embracing us with emotions

We eventually cool down

Finishing our sangrias that were streaming beads of sweat

Like your love trickling down the side of my heart

I softly kiss you, goodbye

Holding you close

Looking forward to the day

We will share Sangrias again

Thoughts of a Closet Freak

Gummy Necklace

The strawberry candles twinkle in the dark
While the silhouette of her body follows her
As she seductively approaches him

He is sitting at the kitchen table
Twirling the mascot in his wine glass
Licking his lips

Her red lace bra, garters, and fishnet stockings
Placed just right
Match her red strappy stilettos

Gifts of Seduction

The soothing sound of R&B music plays softly in the distance

As she sensually straddles him

Wearing a multi-flavored gummy necklace

She gently leans forward

So, he can take a bite..

Thoughts of a Closet Freak

Seductive Feathers and a Blindfold

One warm summer night,
A woman wearing a sexy black dress
Takes her man's hand

Leading him to a soft red velvet chair
To share with him something new

Her black satin gloves
Were soft to the touch

The excitement in his eyes was priceless
As she slips a satin blindfold over his eyes

Gifts of Seduction

They laugh

Confirming this is safe

The conversation stops

As a saxophone plays faintly in the distance

She stands in front of him

With one of his legs slightly in between hers

Close enough for him to feel her presence

But far enough away for him to wonder what was next

She takes her wand of black feathers

Softly slithering them across the top of his bold head

Down the side of his face

Thoughts of a Closet Freak

He slightly exhales to the touch
While the feathers glide down his chest

She removes the feather from his skin
Creating a silent wonder

Then gently trickles the feathers down
The other side of his face

Gently leaning forward
She whispers sweet nothings into his ear
As her breasts press against his chest

She slithers down his body
Kneeling in front of him

Draping the feathers down his arms

Across his boxers

Around his legs

Down to his feet

She moves her satin gloves

Up his chest

Around his neck

Circling behind his head

Removing the blindfold

He was enchanted

Staring into her eyes

Gently picking her up

To devour her

Intertwined

A pair of souls meet

Joining their lips

As their bodies entangle

Fulfilling each other's desires

Causing the friction between their skin to ignite

As they begin to perspire

The sweat trickles down their bodies

Like rain streaming down the windowpane

They simultaneously moan for more

As their bodies become one

Slowly untangling themselves

But never completely letting go

Of their burning passion for each other

Thoughts of a Closet Freak

Assume the Position

A passionate glance caught her attention

As she walks to the kitchen

Biting her lip, smiling

Her body knows exactly what that look means

And what's about to go down

He follows her to the kitchen

Hugging her from behind

Whispering in her ear

She slightly leans forward, up against the counter

Wasting no time

He slides in

Gripping her hips from behind

He moves one hand up her chest

Bringing her close

Gliding his other hand up around her neck

Turning her head to kiss him

They breath heavily as the pressure increases

Every time she assumes the position

Thoughts of a Closet Freak

Chocolate Painting Pleasure

A gameboard

Four small paintbrushes

With little glass jars filled with chocolate flavoring

Laying on a soft blanket in front of the fireplace

A curious couple sits down, snuggling close

Ready to explore what this game has in store

The first roll of the dice

He lands on a chocolate square

With a smile, he turns over a chocolate card

Showing an image of a neck with a heart

She pulls her hair up

He dips the paintbrush into the white chocolate

Gently painting a heart on her neck

She lets out a slight giggle

From the soft brush bristles

He puts the brush back with a smile

Now it's his turn to lick the heart away

Once again, tickling her neck with each stroke

This time, she is breathless

With anticipation in her eyes

She rolls the dice

Landing on a dare square

In wonder, she turns over the dare card

Showing the words "Paint Anywhere"

Thoughts of a Closet Freak

He rubs his hands together, biting his bottom lip
Lightly dips a new brush into the strawberry chocolate
She kisses the brush and pulls him close
Massaging her strawberry lips onto his earlobe

He moans from the warmth of her lips
Relaxing from the massaging of her tongue
He pulls her close, rubbing her back
Staying longer than expected

He attempts to pick up the dice
But the body dessert was too hard to resist
Leaving more chocolate tasting for next time

Classy Cuffs

Click clack

Click clack

Goes the fuzzy red handcuffs

Around her wrists and the arms of the chair

He tells her to relax

While she takes a deep breath

He stands in front of her wearing black satin boxers

His six-pack glistening in the candlelight

He kneels down

Spreading her legs

To get a taste

Thoughts of a Closet Freak

She exhales in pure pleasure

Enjoying every minute

He occasionally massages her breasts

Softly touching inside her body

As she drips down his hand onto the floor

She is going crazy

Kindly begging him to let her feel him

With a friendly grin

He takes the keys off the table

Unlocking the handcuff

One by one

The Only Benefit

Sipping some wine on a Saturday evening

Yearning to feel the touch of someone familiar

She scrolls through her phone

Checking the last time they connected

Hesitantly, she sends a text

And just like that, there he is

Always ready to please

Thoughts of a Closet Freak

Together in the Warmth

Coming home from a long day
Drained and fatigued
He walks into the bathroom

His clean boxers are placed on a towel
With a hot bath awaiting his entrance

She is standing in her birthday suit
With a smile, kissing his lips
Gently removing his shirt

Her hands find their way down his tattooed chest
Unbuttoning and removing his pants

She escorts him to their oversized jacuzzi tub
Made for two

He holds her hand
Assisting her into the bubbles
As he carefully follows

Sitting side by side
Relaxing with their eyes closed

Listening to the subtly waterfall sounds
Playing so in the distance
With a calming aroma of lavender and vanilla candles
Burning all around them

Thoughts of a Closet Freak

After a few minutes of relaxation

He opens his eyes

To his surprise

She hands him a wine glass

With raspberries floating at the top

They toast to the happiness that love brings

Enjoying the moments

They cherish together

The warmth of the water calming their spirits

One sip at a time

She lies on his chest while he holds her close

Making the weekly grind of life worth living

Candle Wax of Love

The light flickers

Sparking the Hawaiian breeze massage candle

While she is patiently waiting for it to melt

She lays him face down on the bed

Startling him

Gently removing his shirt

The wax gradually liquefies into a warm puddle

Carefully and slowly

She trickles the melted candle wax down the middle of his back

He inhales in surprise

Not expecting the warm sensation

Thoughts of a Closet Freak

With both hands massaging into the wax
They glide up his spine
Pressing on his back muscles
Working their way up to his neck

He exhales
Completely relaxing
Melting to the touch of her hands
As they glide up and down his back

She leans forward to massage the sides of his neck
Resting her dangling necklaces
Between his shoulder blades

She lies on his back
Massaging his right earlobe with her tongue
Tracing her fingertips around his head

Gifts of Seduction

She slides her arms under him
Embracing his chest
With her face next to his
Whispering, "Turnover"

While she is still straddling him
He turns over very carefully
Staring into her eyes

Her skin glistens in the candlelight
With her long curly hair draping on the outsides of her breasts

She pours the hot wax into her hand
Cooling it down as she rubs her hands together

She begins massaging his stomach and chest
In a long circular motion

Thoughts of a Closet Freak

As she approaches his neck

Her beautiful breasts are pressed together by her arms

Her eyes captivate him

With a passionate irresistible look

Firmly massaging, while arching his neck

He closes his eyes

Melting into her hands

Thirsty Thrill

She leans back up against the hotel headboard
Watching her man devour her
Enjoying the pleasure he brings

Beads of sweat start trickling down their bodies
So, she grabs the liquor bottle from the nightstand
To quench her thirst

Wanting to share the refreshing taste
She leans her head back
Slowly pours the liquor down between her breasts

He catches a slight taste
Getting turned on by the spontaneous gesture

Thoughts of a Closet Freak

>He gazes up at her
>Latching on a little tighter
>Licking her a little faster
>Touching her a little deeper

Water Works

He lifts her up

Setting her naked body on the dinning room table

Kissing her softly

Sliding his fingers in

Penetrating a spot she had not felt before

She tries to pull his hand away

But he whispers in her ear to trust him

She leans back

Embraces the moment

Allowing herself to release a new water

Squirting all over him

Thoughts of a Closet Freak

With her love streaming down his legs

Dripping off the table onto the floor

The water keeps coming

Giving her a relief only the right person could bring

A Movie and Popcorn

The camera is set on the tripod

The cords are connected

The screen is on

Our popcorn is popped

Waiting for the movie to start

We dim the lights

As the red button flashes on

The camera of passion starts

We watch every inch live

As we create an erotic experience

Only for us to see

In the Midst of You

Sitting together in the car
Ready to explore the nightlife

You light up before we go inside
Inhaling the relaxation of life into your lungs

I look over
Staring into the soul of the man I love

The smoke slowly flows out of your mouth
As you stare back at me through the clouds

Ignoring the world around us
I lean over into the driver's seat
Kissing you as I unbutton your pants

Gifts of Seduction

Stroking you

Peening to make you want me

I slither down

Placing you in my mouth

In surprise, you hold my hair

Exhaling, enjoying the massage

After a few minutes, you tell me to stop

Or we will not make it inside

I sit up

Whipping my mouth

Smiling with a slight giggle

Making the playing field even

You lean into my seat

Touching me softly

Thoughts of a Closet Freak

As you taste my candy

I start overflowing onto the seat

Trying to resist giving in

I stop you from moving my chair back any further

You sit up, with no hesitation

Drive your car to the back of the parking lot

You get out with your pants unbuttoned

Hopping into the back seat

Smoothly telling me to come warm you up

I happily crawl over the seat

Taking off my pants

Resting my feet on the front seat headrest

I hold your waist

Guiding you into the warmth you desire

The windows start to steam up

The hotter our bodies get

Trying to hurry before we get caught

Making the adventure unforgettable

Thoughts of a Closet Freak

Going Up

The city parking garage was full

While we drove around and around

Looking for a parking spot

Finally, someone was leaving right next to the elevator

My husband speeds up to get the space

Excited to meet our friends

I check my makeup in the mirror

Touching up my lip gloss

Before we get out of the car

It is a very cold March night in Seattle

We rush to the elevator

Gifts of Seduction

The doors open

No one is inside

Sparking a naughty idea

I enter quickly

In my strappy high heels

Short black fitted dress

And lean into the corner, biting my bottom lip

My husband walks in after me

With a hunger in his eyes

Unbuttoning his jeans

I push the button to close the doors faster

Select the breezeway level bottom as our destination

Then pull up my dress

And put my arms around his neck

As he picks me up

Thoughts of a Closet Freak

With my legs dangling over his strong forearms

He moves my panties to the side

Talking dirty in my ear

We steam up the elevator

Enjoying the moment

Trying to be quiet

All of a sudden,

The elevator door dings

Before we reach our stop

I frantically try to adjust my panties

Pulling down my dress

But the doors open

Four college kids are standing there

They walk into the elevator

Minding their own business

Without a care in the world

I look at my husband

Only to see his ass was out, sitting on the handrail

I look forward

Trying my best not to laugh

While he nonchalantly fixes his pants

When the kids realize what we were doing

They start smiling

Looking at each other, whispering

The awkward silence continues to build

One garage level at a time

Thoughts of a Closet Freak

Finally,

The doors open to the breezeway entrance

The kids move to the side

We walk out laughing while he buttons his pants

As the elevator doors shut behind us

He grabs my hand

Leading me down the breezeway

Where our friends are happily waving at us to hurry up

Behind the Satin Bow

There was a knock at his door

Not expecting his girlfriend for another hour

He asks who it is

She laughs and tells him to open the door

To his surprise

She was wearing a navy blue and white striped peacoat

Closed with a white satin bow

Standing with her legs crossed

In some nude strappy heels

With her hands in her pockets

Thoughts of a Closet Freak

She unties the white satin bow

Propping her left hand high on the doorframe

Allowing her jacket to drape open

Revealing her sleek satin navy-blue bra and pants

Twirling a piece of her straight brown hair around her finger

Mesmerized by her beauty

Ready for whatever she has in store

He eagerly grabs each side of her open jacket

Pulling her inside

Swiftly shutting the door behind her

A Night of Seduction

He opens the bedroom door

Looking to his right

There she is

Standing in the bathroom doorway

Wearing a short white babydoll nightie

With a fluffy white boa

Draped around her neck

Her long, soft, straight blonde hair is tied up

With a white satin scarf

He closes the door

Sitting on the edge of the bed

Thoughts of a Closet Freak

She walks towards him

In her white fluffy high heel slippers

Twirling the right end of her boa in a circle

The dim light from the fireplace crackling in the distance

Outlines her body with a gentle glow

Catching shimmering glimpses of

Her long-layered diamond necklace

Intrigued by her sexiness

He touches her smooth skin

She passionately takes off his white tank top

Tossing it onto the floor

Her hands rub his shoulders

Moving around the back of his neck

She leans him back onto the bed
Resting his head on a pillow

Time stands still
As he watches her crawl on top of him
Gently straddling him
She begins massaging his neck with her tongue

He glides his hands down her back
As she moves to his soft lips
Kissing and sucking them delicately

She slithers her tongue down his chest
Kisses around his lower stomach
Then placing her mouth around him

Thoughts of a Closet Freak

With her hand and mouth moving together

He softly moans for more

She slowly climbs back on top

Gliding down on him

Shifting her hips back and forth

Pressing her chest against his

She wraps her arm around his neck

To get a better grip

Softly biting his earlobe

He firmly grabs her ass

As it pounds against him

She whispers her desire to switch positions

He is ready

Slithering down to please her

She instantly grabs the pillows

As the touching and licking continues

Her breath gets shorter and louder

He eventually stops

Standing up, licking his sexy brown lips

He places her legs over his arms

Sliding in

Her body instantly feels the pressure

As he leans in

Holding her tight

Thoughts of a Closet Freak

Lightly pulling her hair
Telling her how much he loves her
They gaze into each other's eyes
Enjoying the connection
Embracing their eternal flame

Lunchtime Sounds

She opens his office door

Swiftly locking it behind her

Surprised to see her

Greeting her with a hug

She puts her finger in front of her lips

Politely requesting silence

She puts her hands on his chest

Moving him backwards

Laying him back on his desk

She lifts up her skirt

Unzips his suit pants

Sliding on top of him

Gliding up and down

Thoughts of a Closet Freak

He caresses her body

As she holds him close

Trying not to knock anything off his desk

He brings his chest to hers

Embracing her tightly

Picking her up

Wrapping her legs around his waist

Carrying her to the wall

He starts penetrating her

Whispering to her not to make a sound

The connection immediately ignites

Exploding with pleasure

Kissing quickly as they get dressed

She whispers sweet nothings

Secretly knowing

She will be surprising him again for lunch next week

Something New

I lay back on the edge of the bed

Enjoying the passion

Slow and long

In and out

Teasing me with every stroke

Holding my legs over your strong forearms

I began touching myself to increase the sensation

You move my feet around your neck

Slightly leaning forward

Thoughts of a Closet Freak

Gliding your right hand up my chest
Gently grabbing my neck
I touch your hand to control the pressure

With your left hand gripping my hip
Widening your stance to go deeper
You start putting in the work

With a little pressure and pain
You let your love rain down on me

Secrets from Within

Thoughts of a Closet Freak

Unexpected Interruption

During the daily morning meeting
Her imagination starts roaming

What would happen if I acted on his advances
On a quiet Saturday evening…

He would open the door, look around
Only to find her standing at the top of the stairs

She is wearing a short, red, fuzzy bathrobe
Revealing her sexy black thigh highs and garter belt
In her red bottom heels

Secrets from Within

Her soft brown hair tied up in a satin ponytail scarf
As her vanilla skin shimmers in the candlelight

He slowly walks up the stairs
Finally touching her hand
She leads him to the bedroom

The aroma of roses fills the air
The red LED light glows in the background
While their shadows silhouette through the window

They passionately undress each other
As his body grows longer
She gets wetter

Thoughts of a Closet Freak

She whispers her desire to feel him

He lays her on her back

Climbing on top

Her body instantly throbs for more

As he strokes her spot

He holds her tightly

Tearing down her walls

Reaching ecstasy as one

They slowly relax

Get dressed and kiss goodbye…

As the meeting ends,

She snaps back to reality

Ready to tackle the day

Wondering where that unexpected fantasy came from

Caught in the Middle

Do I be myself,

Or do what he is demanding?

Even if it hurts me.

Do I stay true,

Or pretend to like it?

Out of fear of losing him.

Do I deny my desires,

Or express them?

Even if they don't turn him on.

Do I stay in a box,

Or free myself?

To be the sexual person I hide inside.

Thoughts of a Closet Freak

The Gaze from Within

When you gaze into my eyes

I once saw a person

Who loved me unconditionally

Always capturing my heart at hello

When you gaze into my eyes

I once felt a person

That explored my sexual desires

Giving me the energy to try new things

Allowing me to trust

Feeling safe in your arms

Over time,

Your gaze has become crystal clear

I learned you were a person

Who could love me one day

Then swiftly turn into a witty, narcissistic man

Filled with a spiteful spirit the next

Your gaze has become consistently inconsistent

I learned to stop believing a person

Who could trust my word

But lie to me regularly with no hesitation

Knowing I could read him like a book

Your gaze has become a disconnected memory

I learned to erase my feelings for a person

Who could not make sound choices

Removing the sexual connection once undeniable for us both

Thoughts of a Closet Freak

A Man I Once Craved

When I was younger,

You were someone

That made me smile at the thought of you

You were someone

That made me happy with the sound of your voice

You were someone

That loved spending time with me all day, every day

You were someone

That touched my body in a way no one else could

You were someone

That stole my heart, holding me hostage for years

As I grew into a strong woman,

I became someone

You threw to the wayside

When I needed you

I became someone

You allowed others to talk down about

When we were supposed to be a team

I became someone

You stopped loving, with every devastating disappointment

I started experiencing

I became someone

You tried to devalue, with no accountability for your actions

Burning the bridges, we tried to rebuild

I became a stranger

To the one I once called my husband

Thoughts of a Closet Freak

Love's Shackled Prisoner

Sitting home alone like a prisoner
Waiting for you to come back

To care about me
To love me
The way you once did

The shackles of love weighing me down
Keeping me from moving forward
Staying loyal to the love we used to make
A touch I craved only from you

One day,

I will have the strength to break free

Removing the love from my heart

Finding the courage to pack up my life

Walking away from our house that was never a home

Trusting I will survive

Breaking free from my trauma bonds

To your body

Our souls

The family

I only wanted to share with you

Thoughts of a Closet Freak

Shattered Glass

The sledgehammer struck her heart

Fiercely with no warning

It shattered like a glass vase

Into a million pieces

She lay on the floor, lifeless, and in shock

Trying to recover from the blow

She slowly regains her breath

Starting to pick up the pieces

Some were large and easy to see

While others were invisible, cutting her skin

Secrets from Within

There were still a few slivers of her heart
She could never find

She searched for years
But those pieces of her heart were never the same
Still bleeding in silence

Until one day,
She looked in the mirror
Her lost pieces were the most important
But the hardest to see

Her reflection reminded her that
Self-worth, forgiveness, and love
Were the shattered pieces she had to heal
On her own from within

Thoughts of a Closet Freak

Trusting the One We Follow

As a little girl

I could not wait to meet the man of my dreams

Someone who

I went to school with

Grew up with

Could have an extended family to be a part of

A man

I would marry

Build a home with

Filling it with happy children

Together as one

However

When we make our choices without God

Sometimes our plans

Turn into harsh life lessons

That scare us forever

Bringing us back

To the spirit, the word, and the guidance we seek

Helping us survive and overcome

The choices we made without him

Callus

The anxiety swells in her chest
As another day goes by
Trying to ignore the silence of her phone

Her heart aches with temporary disappointment
Enduring sleepless nights

Questioning her choice to take a chance
Allowing herself the freedom to feel affection
For someone she cared for

Only to be swiftly reminded
Why her heart is hardened
Becoming immune to the fairy tales of love

Not Enough

My intelligence is intriguing, but not worth enough

To keep your interest

When I want to learn about you

My time is desired, but not valuable enough

For you to organize a date

When I say I need to plan

My body is sexy, but not respected enough

To keep your attention

When I choose to get to know you first

My face is beautiful, but not captivating enough

To keep you consistently engaged

When you have options with no strings attached

The Silent Daily Reminders

Two kids

One mom

Together as a family

Guided by a pillar of strength

Even when she feels alone

With the sunshine around her heart fading

Losing hope from the storms life brings

Two Divorces

One decision

To lead a healthy home

Empowered by the accountability to stand alone

Even when she doesn't know how

With the financial burden for her kids alone

Motivating her to strive for greatness

Two smiles

One love

A reflection of happiness

Dedicated to leading by example

Ensuring her children know the meaning of true love

Sacrificing her needs and desires

To build a legacy worth following

Thoughts of a Closet Freak

The Wedge of Life

She stays the night at his house
For the first time in months

Surprising her with a candlelight dinner for two
With smooth R&B playing in the background

After they exchange a few kisses
He presents her with a key to his place
Surprised he was moving so fast
She hesitantly took the key

They chatted in the candlelight
Slow dancing to a few songs
The moments were heating up
As he led her to his bedroom

Secrets from Within

He had a surprise for her
They each took quick showers separately
Meeting back in his room

He pulls a sex wedge out of the closet
Putting it on the bed
She was excited
As the last wedge she tried set a standard

He tells her to come over
Leaning her face down on the edge
Elevating her hips higher than normal
He gently massages her butt cheeks while he slides in

Thoughts of a Closet Freak

Waiting for the moment to heat up
Anticipating a night of pleasure
Wanting something new

He does not hold it
And it was over

She was dumbfounded
Slowly leaning up to move the wedge out of the way
She let him know she was not pleased

With a smile on his face and a chuckle in his voice
He told her that was it

With irritation in her heart
She knew being unsatisfied was unacceptable long term

Secrets from Within

Waking up early before him
Getting dressed silently

She slowly sneaks out the front door
Mailing his house key back
Never to return again

Thoughts of a Closet Freak

The Lonely World of Boundaries

Over time we build boundaries

From the harsh lessons life brings

Protecting us from the red flags, we once chose to ignore

Boundaries allow us to accept the actions people show us as truth

Instead of playing the victim and asking ourselves why

Requiring us to set standards upfront

Before we get attached to a person who is not ready to build

Driving us to control feelings that overpower our judgment

Opening our hearts to the devastation of disappointment

Causing us to sacrifice our impulses for affection

To confirm their intentions, align with ours

Sometimes boundaries can leave us lonely

But keep us mindful of protecting our peace

One to Remember

A man who has touched your soul

Is a man you never forget

The passion he expresses when he looks into your eyes

Caressing your heart one blink at a time

With a confident gaze that confirms your connection

Building a trust, you never felt

The kindness he shows

When he messages your body

Holding you close

With the feeling he will never let you go

Thoughts of a Closet Freak

Exhale

"Ahhuuhh"

"Hummmm"

She can barely control herself

Losing her breath

Overtaken by the pleasure he brings

"Baby, don't move"

"I'm not ready"

She tightens her legs around his waste

Stopping him for a moment

To hold him inside, not wanting it to end

He leans forward onto her breasts
Wrapping his muscular arm behind her neck

Kissing her slowly, he slides his hand under her butt
Tilting her hips up

Holding her in place, he gently starts penetrating her
This time, the sensation is so intense
All she can do is exhale

"AHHH"
"You feel so good"
"I'm going to come"
"AHHH"

Thoughts of a Closet Freak

Lioness in the Shadows

She is sipping her margarita at the bar
Enjoying the music and laughter
Spending time with friends

Slightly gazing around the room
From time to time
To see if there is someone
Worth fantasizing about from afar

Unexpectedly, a sexy man caught her eye
His swag was on point
Hair freshly cut
With a smile as captivating as his presence

Secrets from Within

She mingles with her family
Acting as if she doesn't notice him
She notices him whispering to her cousin
While he was looking her way

Eventually, her cousin introduces them
Shaking his hand firmly
She smiles, matching his energy

His intelligence intrigues her curiosity
But she knows his type

She pulls away, creating distance
To observe his intentions

Her prowling nature grows inside
As she catches him gazing her way

Thoughts of a Closet Freak

Her body was attracted

Staring into the distance

Fixating on wanting to feel their connection

The thought of taking him home swirls in her mind

Turning on her favorite sexy playlists

Lighting her Hawaiian Breeze candies

As they make margaritas together in the shadows

Sitting him at the table

Only to disappear for a moment

Slipping into a short black see-through dress

Entering the room

He looks up in surprise, rubbing his hands together

Secrets from Within

She starts to dance

Letting the music speak through her body

As she walks behind him

Sliding her hands down his chest

Breathing gently

Grazing his earlobe with her tongue

His heart beats faster and stronger in anticipation...

Suddenly he approaches her at the bar

Asking what she was thinking about so deeply

She laughs trying to compose herself

Realizing she was in a prowling trance

Craving a feeling to devour him only in her mind

Untouchable

We share story after story

Past lovers and heartaches

Successes and mistakes

Trying to understand how our pasts have shaped us

Ensuring we invest enough time to take a risk

We will not regret

Voluntarily sharing my sexual experiences

To teach you why I have fears trusting

In efforts to show you how to keep me present

Secrets from Within

One day,

Maybe allowing myself to open up

Acting on my desires

Fulfilling yours

Committing to something

I won't have to let go

Can't Wait

I can't wait

To unleash my desires

Expressing the love

I want to share

I can't wait

To caress his skin

Providing the security

I want to receive

I can't wait

To get the business

Receiving the passion

I want to return

I can't wait

To do it over and over again

Experiencing the ecstasy

I want to enjoy

Unforgettable

Unexpected Connection

As we greeted one another
Your politeness was noticed

As you spoke
Your words made me feel safe

As our legs casually touched under the table
I felt connected

As your charming confidence
Refreshed my spirit, I felt free to be myself

As your brown eyes unexpectedly drew me in
Your soft kiss felt secure

Unforgettable

As you pulled me close
Your embrace felt genuine

As you walked me to my car
Our hands softly intertwined

As we stood in the rain, kissing
You picked me up, wrapping my legs around you
Filling my heart with excitement

As our encounter, in the rain, was unexpected
I felt alive, wanting more

As I softly wiped the water from your bald head
We kissed goodbye

Driving away with butterflies in my stomach
Anticipating our next unexpected connection

Thoughts of a Closet Freak

Undercover Love

You are the flame to my fire

With just a spark

You ignite a love

That swarms through my body

A feeling that makes me throb

You are the ice cube in my water

With just a drop

You quench my thirst

Cooling my mind

Unleashing a craving that makes me wet

Unforgettable

You are my star in the night

With just a glow

You guide the way

Leading me back to you

A magnetic irresistible desire

You are the Pandora in my box

With a fantasy

You bring out my deepest desires

That connect our hearts

A bond that replays in my mind

The Touch

Your hands make my heart melt

The moment you touch me

The softness of your lips

Takes my breath away

Your muscular chest on top of me

Warms my breasts

The feeling of your body inside mine

Intertwines our love

Touching a part of me

Only you can find

Reminiscing

The music

Brought a smile to my face

Reminding me

Of the love we made

Even though

Those times are over

The memories of us

Last forever

Until Next Time

When we connect, it's magical
Capturing our hearts every time

Our eyes read each other's minds
Never missing a moment

Our bodies moving in perfect harmony
Making a song only we hear

A never-ending connection
Entangling us forever

We may part ways
But never say goodbye
To the passion in our hearts

Unforgettable

We silently spent months and years
Missing the love, we shared

Trying to fill a void
Only you can fill for me
And I can fill for you

So, we patiently wait
Until one of us picks up the phone
And we meet again

The Heart's Assumption

Once we see each other, the passion burns deep
The rare experience of what true love feels like
A commitment we thought was forever

Making us temporarily suppress the reasons we left
Hoping our rekindled love would keep us together
Without healing the scars, we inflicted
Pretending we truly forgave each other

The resentment and lack of growth
Reminds our hearts
Never to assume the passion we crave for each other
Will keep us together

After Thoughts

Thoughts of a Closet Freak

Double Standard

Refuse to be labeled
As less than

Hold your head high
Look towards the sky

Thankful you choose love
The path to peace

Honoring the freedom to fly
Growing your spirit

Fulfilling a destiny
Designing only for you

Hard Lesson Learned

He was charming

Spending many long nights

Falling asleep on the phone with me

He finally comes to town

Taking me on a romantic dinner

Staying up most of the night talking

Sipping on an orange drink with a splash of liquor

I started feeling nauseous

Apologizing for my sudden sickness

I ask permission to take a nap on his bed for a moment

Thoughts of a Closet Freak

In a caring manor, he agrees
Apologizing for my condition

Not knowing how long I was out
I wake up to him on top of me and my pants off

I was not expecting this from him
Nor did I intend to give him this impression

I was not in a state to defend myself
And realizing this could go sideways
I went along with it
Then went to sleep

In the morning
There were no hard feelings
But I knew
I would never let that happen again

After Thoughts

Forgiveness is Freedom

Forgive others for the hurt
To free our minds from the trauma

Forgive others for the pain
Sexually inflicted upon us by force

Forgive others for the misunderstandings
Casting us in a dark light
To free ourselves from the judgment of others

Gifting ourselves the strength to overcome
The mistakes that once defined us

Thoughts of a Closet Freak

Be True

The only person

In the way of your self-worth is you

So, step aside

Quiet doubting yourself

Ignore your fears of being alone

Take time to reflect on your sexual encounters

Why you allowed yourself to be vulnerable

Understand why you sacrifice your desires

Just to save a relationship

After Thoughts

Learn from the mistakes that have defined you

To free yourself from your past

No longer playing a victim to bad relationships

But knowing and resisting the red flags

Protecting your peace for the relationship

You deserve

Sexual Soul Ties

Bonds her to other people's souls

Creating connections

She can't erase

Requiring her to heal from the disappointment

To once again trust being vulnerable to another

Risking a possible future severed connection

She can't afford to endure

So, she learns over time

How to disconnect her soul from vulnerability

After Thoughts

They may replay those moments of her

Over and over

Keeping them a secret

Or sharing them with friends

But her need to keep her ties to their soul

Becomes a distant feeling of the past

Using the random encounters

For an opportunity

Allowing herself to feel

Releasing the sexual person locked inside her heart

The Morning Drive Home

As I drive home from your house

I reminisce about what we shared

The dancing we enjoyed

The laughter we shared

The way our bodies spoke to each other

And the beginning to a friendship that seemed effortless

Suddenly, an unerasable smile brightened my spirit

My stomach filled with butterflies

As I remembered what it was like to feel again

Just for a moment

After Thoughts

Until I realized that the way you said goodbye
Let me know that was our last time

A little part of me was hurt
But I don't regret our soulful connections
That will occasionally replay in the back of my mind

Thoughts of a Closet Freak

Sex vs Love

Sex is disconnected

Reminding us not to get involved

Just to enjoy a temporary feeling

That has addictive consequences

We look to someone else to fulfill

Love is a bond

Willingly tying our souls together

Creating a predictable and magical utopia

Confirming a level of security

To someone we can trust without asking

After Thoughts

Two Halves Don't Make a Whole

Two halves are broken people

Trying to fill voids with one another

Never succeeding together

Because part of them is broken

Wrestling with a past they have not accepted

But two whole people

Coming together makes a couple

Standing together strong

Loving each other as one

Single Satisfaction

Being single is safe
Predictable

Providing a place of peace
With no distractions
Just self-reflection and acceptance

A way to preserve your body
For the one it is meant for
Not all that apply

After Thoughts

Saving Yourself

Exploring the oceans to find the right captain

Doesn't mean we have to swim in all waters

Watching the ships go by

Teaches you how to spot the captain

That will weigh you down

Observing what they have on board

Shows you the fruits you may bear

Or the diseases you will receive

Taking the time to learn the ropes

Puts you with a captain who will

Lead you to the promise land, not blow wind in your sails

So, keep a steady eye

Waiting for the ship possessing longevity and love

Thoughts of a Closet Freak

The True Love of Another

As you get older

The desires for connection, affection, and love never fade

They just look different

When a man looks into my eyes

Truly seeing me

My heart learns to trust him

Allowing me to try new positions

Fulfilling his desires

Seeing him work hard

Providing for our family

Improving our lives for the better

Turns me on

Every time he walks through the door

After Thoughts

Helping with the kids
Cooking together
Strengthening us
Makes my body feen for him
Anytime, anyplace

Trusting that he can lead me
Guiding our family to success
Is unmeasurable to the level of affection
I can show in return

About the Author

I was born in Tacoma, Washington, raised by my parents and with my older sister. A month before graduating high school, I got drunk for my first time with a guy I had a crush on and he non-violently raped me when I was passed out. A few years after, I confronted him and he apologized. However, that experience did curve my ability to trust men sexually for years. I learned how to forgive and repair myself so I would be able to enjoy my sexual desires with someone.

I never wanted to have other partners as I was saving myself for marriage. However, life has its way of teaching us valuable lessons about ourselves, moving forward, and how to set healthy sexual boundaries. I did not date much before I had my son at twenty-two. I got married, divorced twice, and am now a woman over forty, experiencing dating in today's world, which is eye-opening. It requires boundaries and learning how to be happy alone. This has taught me to be sexually selective and how to refrain from my desires in order to keep my peace.

Sex and love are things we all deserve to experience and enjoy. Never hold back your inner curiosity and desires because of others. Find the right person who will allow you to trust them with your sexual secrets and set yourself free. Do not be afraid to educate yourself and learn how to do new things. You will be amazed at what the right person will bring into your life.

Thank You

Thank you for spending your time in my thoughts.
I would love to hear from you.
Connect with me on social media.
Instagram: @Thoughtsoflisarenee
LinkedIn, Facebook, and TikTok: Author Lisa Renee Hutchins
YouTube: Thoughts of Lisa Renee Hutchins – Author
Email: thoughtsoflisarenee@gmail.com
www.authorlisareneehutchins.com

Stay amazing and don't let your past define you!
It is only a lesson learned on your journey to greatness!

www.ingramcontent.com/pod-product-compliance
Lightning Source LLC
Chambersburg PA
CBHW070801100426
42742CB00012B/2217